To Curve

Also by Michael Daley

Books
The Straits
Way Out There: Lyrical Essays

Chapbooks
Angels
Amigos
Yes, Five Poems
Original Sin
The Corn Maiden
Rosehip Plum Cherry

Edited
Dalmo'ma 1 & 2
In Our Hearts & Minds: The Northwest & Central America

Translation
Horace: Eleven Odes

To Curve

Poems by Michael Daley

Word Press

for Phyllis
Michael Daley

c.1

Published by Word Press
P.O. Box 541106
Cincinnati, OH 45254-1106

ISBN: 9781934999196
LCCN: 2008930533

Poetry Editor: Kevin Walzer
Business Editor: Lori Jareo

Visit us on the web at www.word-press.com

Acknowledgments

Grateful acknowledgments are due the editors of the following publications where many of these poems first appeared in books, chapbooks, anthologies, and magazines: *Alaska Quarterly Review, Anthology of Magazine Verse and Yearbook of American Poetry 1995/1996, Callapooya Collage, Cumberland Review, Dalmo'ma, Empty Bowl, Graham House Review, Hudson Review, Jeopardy, Litrag, Manoa, Nebraska Review, Northwest Passage, Old Dog New Trick, Peace or Perish Anthology, Pleasure Boat Studio, Ploughshares, Poetry East, Poets Voices, Pontoon, Prairie Schooner, Raven Chronicles, Sagittarius Press, Seattle Review, Shadow Marks, Sonoma Stump, Stone House, Tampa Review, Tangram, Waterways, Weathered Pages, Wood Works, Writer's Almanac,* and *10Point five*. My thanks also to Tim McNulty, Finn Wilcox, Mike O'Connor, Steve Clark, Jack Estes, Paul Hunter, and especially Kathy Prunty for their friendship, love and insights which have nurtured this book.

Cover watercolor by Janos Piroska of Csongrad, Hungary, 1894-1987

Author photo by Kathy Prunty

For my Students

Table of Contents

One

Original Sin

My mother waited till now
to hand down this gold razor
her father let slip
in the washbowl.
In a hurry to teamster the horses,
soap on his earlobe and nostril,
he climbed the fire-wagon.
When she poured the wash water
onto pebbles, hard gold
sluiced at the bottom
with the whiskers.
A gold razor, small for travel,
beside the soap,
I wipe a circle in the foggy mirror,
my face doughy and wet,
the age I always am,
burrs sprung on my cheek,
chin, under my lip.
Sister Josephine chalked dots, sins
born inside the circle, the soul.
Death camps originated in Eden.
Abel, the shepherd, was murdered.
I scrape my chin.
Already our baby sees me
as a dot, translucent
on the slippery wall,
shadow on the fetal eyelash,
a whisper, "shit," like my father,
not often, but when he nicked his jaw.
My parents met
packaging Blue Blades
at Gillette's plant on a river
for workers to smooth
their Hellenic chins in the war,
for prisoners and jailers to swap,
for cold fingers sawing the wrist.
I was afraid too.

For me it was sex.
Not the delicate way
I unbutton your dress,
and huddle over the body
inside the body, but once
I saw my parents on their lunch break.
Having merely opened the blouse and pants
like secret lovers, they kept laughing,
and then they whispered when they came.
They went back to work. That was my sin:
shadow in shadow, riding the dark water,
I didn't know my father and mother
were in love, and young, happy,
skinny like me.

After That

When Kadee was a kid and didn't talk,
I used to rock her in the dark
between our parents' bedpost and the crib
to hear her breathe. Now I hold my breath
as they bring her to the *mike,*
as the singer turns, smiles to the keyboard,
and my mother's lips at the dim table move,
a pink streamer tacked up to the ceiling
already free of its tape,
an inch of tattered crepe
dangling from the last "E" of her name.
She's embarrassed, not by the song
(*Jesus—that brightened the whole rotten night),*
but that neighbors could see her—
relations, waitress friends from years
at Blinstrub's, The Beachcomber, The Pony Room,
strangers could touch her hands,
smile across tables spotty with beer.

A month ago, a black stitch still down her back,
my mother was crying in the dark a small
night nurse told me, and I had never, all
my life never seen her tears. Housing
had come to tear the old house down.
But now my sister is grinning,
the brushes pass over the drum.
The moon comes through a corner window.
She sings *YOU* on the air, and
LIGHT UP full of breath, pauses
to brush away smoke, *MY LIFE* just right.
The drummer's cymbals hush,
gold leaf spilling from a dish.
Near the top stair once she jiggled from the knees,
her right eye opened and closed, and closed
and she spilled. These days she says ,

"I'm not retarded, I have a damaged brain."

None of their eyes are on me
when I take my whiskey over to the door.
After that I wanted to watch
the moon on Wollaston Boulevard
and small waves along the pebbly beach,
but some of the women have twisted round
at tables in the rose haze
to peek at my mother
and the rows of their faces
keep beaming.

My Sister Is a Flight of Birds

I'm standing on ice, a flight of geese
fleeing the moon, skimming the roof,
dampens the air. Seven quiet birds.
I have been saying their names so long
and now I can't remember
what their sudden rising means.
They call on the chill air
and let me be. When I slept, I hoped
never to wake and write these poems.
I'm not the man for this.
I wanted fire whispering over pages,
glowing in cloud. Instead,
I have spent my life as a man ice-fishing.
My line jigs down a hole
and sometimes in winter dawn
I draw up one freezing fish, and I'm surprised
holding it out, my glasses fogged like Dad's
under the small brim of his hat
on mornings he tightened our skates.
Can you remember anything from childhood?
I only know how ordinary we were,
sliding on the snow.
All night I kept these words beside my head,
white faces of skaters, a few haunted birds.
You've had me all your life, but I live sometimes
without your face, which looks like mine
afloat in an ice-hole, on a broken blue lake.

My Mother & Me Waiting in the Dark Beside the Beaver Valley Store

Headlights of a pickup
bounce along the road.
Two yellow tractors
sink into a field.
Up the pit a mile
my white car shines
just from rain.
We're staring at the gas pumps.
At home, a warm bath opens its heart.
I like facing these woods with you,
where a dead limb drops in fog,
a car breaks down,
silence keeps going.
Because of you somehow
I am the frail piece of human
I thought I'd never get to be.

A Drop of This

for Maureen

Blue struck the surface
and as though a ribbon
fell through water
released its moonless night
inside my glass.

Have some, he said
under the Cathedral bell
where they fled a drizzle,
his gesture swept space, a stone
square worn by former jailbirds.

Have some. Brutal man,
in whose totalitarian eyes,
privacy clinically revoked,
the glass spills only in the mind.

They dropped through history,
wrist to fist, sipped
the blue delusions,
and all that time,
bells in the rain.

My Father Phones on Sunday

My father phones on Sunday
to speak with the man
who will father his grandson,
but I was just holding his thumb
at Salisbury Beach. The wave
threw my Daddy on the sand,
a finger of sea-foam I swallowed
darkened to blood.
He tells me his weather.
I see bright January
on the rot of his sill,
and the cove I know better than any
place left on earth. Danny
Donovan scraped his arthritic knuckles
on barnacled stone, and Mae the beautiful,
twenty years forgotten by Death,
steps out of weeds
to announce the twenty-first century.
The end of history
arrives on high tide
in the cove I love
where tender grasses moan
under Boston Light,
sails of the arrogant Senators,
and even the Mailman, lost in fog.
How's the weather, my father says.
Raining? Like always? Well, I'll see ya,
before I can ask again
Come sit in my kitchen,
here where my fingers ache
lugging sea-salted fir
and spruce over the shell
of this other, far coast.
The trail washed out,
his hip with the pin
so painful he'll fall,
I'll carry him down on my back,

my father Anchises,
fleeing in flames
the city that bore us.
Iron hands on my shoulders,
I'll never give him up.

Black Lid

A man is out walking hatless after snow by the river,
deep longing, calm the eyes in cars avoid.
He thinks he's watching a heron: long grassy neck
perched on the dry end of a log in the rapid.
It bends its short black trunk. Maybe a loon.
She twists to abandon her purchase,
points her pale bill downriver
—*afraid of me,* he thinks, dark and aimless
stepping from a silence cars provide,
not speaking, not pointing. She bends and shits:
a white spray feathers the surface,
a green cloud in the flood,
and taxis half way across the river
to wash her tail, fanning
as yesterday his takeoff did in ice:
his father's voice three thousand miles ago:
two men stand over a box. The father says
everything you'll need—and all he will have to learn:
Deed, Policies, the Will—filed in a homemade box,
tape and labels on string across the top.
A moment too long they stare into it.
The father shuts the black lid, washes the last dish,
the son puts away the spoon.
I wake up shaking, my mouth frozen as if to weep.
I dreamt I knelt at his cross,
thin medallion strung up in the air.
I wake and pull Teddy out from Kathy's side,
from folds in the dark comforter,
to hold him a moment,
hand on the thatch of his head,
then settle him in the crib
where for the minutes I've gone on writing this,
he thrashes, groans, and is coming painfully awake.

Tears

I'm in my red bathrobe, and he is
out on the sun porch, in tears.
It may be the Scotch—they drank that.
A postcard from after the thirty missions
said "buy a bottle!"
It's dark out there, rectangles of light
from the kitchen windows
disappear among the bark and branches.
Head down, long fingers absently rolling the glass
to and fro, in tears.
I was the peacemaker; I told third grade
how hot tears felt when daddy packs a suitcase
I beg him not to go.
There's been a missed appointment of some kind.
"Your mother didn't give me the message."
He would have been postmaster of our village,
"but for that."

Hemingway calls it Irish inferiority:
grand success followed by despair.
I don't know what I said.
Teen optimism you can bet: fifteen more years
of failure before him.

Months later, in the parking lot
outside The Pony Room, a man with sideburns
walked her to the turquoise Galaxy
my father had just bought for her.
He was driving past,
and an hour later set everything of hers
out on the porch in the rain.
Next day on his soft chairs
we cried because he couldn't find her
and he'd searched every beach for thirty miles.

In the cafeteria today,

late fall light rained on us
and glistened his wheelchair.
At eighty-six the soul has strapped on
its life jacket. Yesterday
they turned him and he cried out.
"I could strangle that doctor with his own
two-hundred dollar tie."
And he cried remembering he carried my grampa
light as a bird, up the stair.

Nothing Can Wash It Away

On a star-lit table, the coleus and aloe
quiver in a dark breeze.
Hardwood creaks under my hip,
a thin mat on the floor
Marie, my good friend,
offered me tonight.
Tomorrow, I sing myself to sleep,
tomorrow I shall leave this town.
Cars send up sheets of light,
voices as from under a sea.
And then a bar of light below Marie's door,
and yelling; her strong frightened voice
wants him to go, a heavy falling noise,
and then he slaps her. "Stop it! Stop it! Stop!"
her roommate screams outside the door,
and pounds her fist, whose own boyfriend
I imagine sits in their bed, folds his hands,
and, with me, shuts his eyes.

Once, when I trembled down my bunk ladder,
tan cowboy pajamas mapping me to a safe prairie,
I stood in the doorway and watched
as if they were framed on the TV,
my mother slapping my father,
but why was he crying, and patting his head?
They fell gracelessly onto the bed.
Its frame collapsed.
She went on hitting.
And years later, another door—
padlocked—where he wrote in crayon:
"I locked you out you sneak thief.
Where's the money you stole from my pocket?"

Nothing can change what I did, Marie.
When I ran down your stairs,
I was thinking about my father in a t-shirt
alone in the big house;

upstairs on the locked door his question
bleeds five coats of paint.
I went outside your house.
I ran in the street.
I paddled with my thumbs
into the whirl of traffic,
until my first ride screamed
behind the taillights
of a silver Barracuda.

My Education

The three-legged turtle limping from clean tank
toward our porch door, shut: ten minutes.
Each claw snags the Berber blooms.
An Anasazi artist designed the gene for carapace.
At the glass door—beak, crimsoned eye,
a penis is his neck—my primate reverence,
the names run off like water.
Scenes from my life go on without me.
A photo of 1949, before memory;
my mother as a teen, I am two.
Is your mother, moccasined or sandaled,
limping this moment into the past?
A breath against my glass door,
shell the blossom trained by what I do not know.
Next life I want to be a swallow.

Fallen

We come now to November.
The sun begs from a weed.
A veil blows off the lake.
Robins, juncos and jays
fatten in uncounted cones.
A sunflower holds up,
from bird-borne or child-dropped
seed, dappled petals, crown
of Indian summer as a Swinomish man,
waist deep with his little wife, called
from the icy Skagit, setting nets
he claims were yesterday robbed,
"How about this Indian Summer?"
Knees purple, an hour at the heater
before driving from the banks.
Yesterday. November 22d, 2 am,
snow 4 inches, her unfinished
stalk bowed by snow, drenched torch
face-down in ice, I sat beside
the sunflower. Thirty years
since Father Cardillo climbed the stairs,
out of breath, and entered American
Literature with Dallas' news,
I sat beside the sunflower.
Snow on the trees across the lake,
their limbs evenly white under moon,
they are delicate membrane immune
as she was, whose statue in the hall
raised perfect broken hands
to Our Lady of Light.
Finally free of heaven
and all other miracles
but happy little earth,
without learning to
my body lies in snow
until it shines with moon
and sinks to the heart of things.

Getting into Heaven

I admit I was the first to wake
inside the long dormitory.
I was ready for moonlight.
During Easter Midnight mass
in a lily's shadow Father Cardillo
strained on a ladder of Gregorian notes,
his voice almost falsetto,
passionate as a man in love.
The year turned off course,
from long nights in northern woods
to brilliant dawn. Later, when the sun knit
the skirt of pine to the window,
I slipped back into chapel
and begged to be lifted too, as he was.
I waited, for the voice, I admit that.
I waited for the perfume of a lily
to saturate these clothes.
Shouts of schoolboys rose from a field.
A wren broke its heart singing.
Jets echoed off the chapel roof.
When I heard earth whistle in space,
I ran down the tilted hall.

Joey Nee

Everything recorded
is scorched onto seed.
You and I walked
with the thin Czech priest
who couldn't name the man
from under whose wing
he fled the concertina wire
to damp forests, ending
with the Roman question,
Cui Bono—for whose good?
What is the use of it?
What good is the past
if you fall in a pit
and close your wing?
Your mother in the projects
isn't watching trains anymore.
A breeze floats sheetrock dust
across her empty sill.
If someone remembered,
I could ask where you are.
The marigold petals
tug a strand of light.
Nowhere, but into this moist grass
where a red ant drags a flea beetle,
am I going to quietly speak your name.

Lucky

And this is the way it was
on days we were stoned all
the time in Highway Eighty's
Illinois corn amazed it is
that tall. The girl tells lies
by the fire, a kid from Toledo
hobbled with jars in a corn row,
swears (near the water pump
where blue police cars go)
he didn't want to jump parole;
they won't take him, will they?
Just for wanting water?
I watch from the corn.
They handcuff him, whip on
flashers, rocket I-80.
Then, we scatter over the husks,
a hound in a panic on the pickup,
megaphones, a farmer's curse,
yellow dust off packs,
embers blowing in the dark.
Her raspy breath behind me—
we've been together since Sunday—
heaves as we run by stars
till only crickets know
we're on the highway
and the trucker—
who beckons from a shimmering cab.
I watch her shoulders slump
when he tells her "Crawl
past that curtain, to my bunk."
Once I knew her name.
I won't remember now.
"Where'd you get her?" "I don't know."
Fields swell together like a sore.
"Here, eat this," a black pill in his palm.
My fingers twine the sleeping bag
I've burrowed in my lap.

He snaps a look across the cab:
thin mustache, greased hair,
white shirt pocket's pearl snap undone,
a pack of *Kools;* offers the hand
twitching on the stick: "Name's Lucky.
Been hauling this shit since Sunday."
He looks ahead at the road.
"And you and me, friend,
we're gonna be up all night."

The Patriarch of an Amish Farm Gave the Bible to a Pilgrim

Why is the song of a cricket
at home in this blue field?
I need that life I burned up yesterday.
The scent of his daughter's berry pie
disappeared in the Shenandoah Valley
where I stopped on the way to my life
to cook a lousy can of beans.
Nights in his weeds I'd mutter to my fist
"You're not going home yet."

I don't care about the earth.
I only mourn it lost from my life;
not that bible, but this cricket.
I worry I'll turn into gray leaf
here in the West, far from my grave.
Where was I going? The highway's noise
is above the pasture's. I will lie
in the shade of a locust, pray
to an indolent cloud, wide as the valley:
" I want you to take me home."

Before Dawn

Foghorns,
shrouded in their heavy working clothes,
call one another.

One moans,
and the other gives back across the warm
heart of town the tone, an octave lower.

The faces of a family
gather at the window of the Laundromat.
Although they're only

beads of steam,
a trick of moon, I refuse to look away.
The smell of old men washed clean humbles me.

I have been awake all night.
A car is parked in the drizzle where the bones
of my face float in a puddle.

In the phone booth a glove I found brushed
against my chin, fingers along my throat.
Starlings call, herons lift off the ferry pilings.

Danny Donovan, drunk, kicking off soaked pants
in the kitchen the night his bilge failed
stood to his waist in muck beside the mooring.

Ten years later, on that gold evening,
his tongue already deserting him, he saw the sea
from his hospital bed;

a boy in a boat
turns from rowing,
a white boat on the gold water.

The foghorn quiet,
a first rooster coughs at the dirt end of night.
My shoes are wet.

Immediately after Announcing Her Upcoming Pre-Cancer Surgery, My Mother Changes the Subject

I just wanted to sit down.
It must have been half past three
or four, and I just wanted to sit
on my couch with my tea
and watch a show. *Oprah*, I think.
I look out my window
here comes Philip running across the street,
a car stops and the driver comes running too.
What's wrong with my house?
What are they looking at?
So I run to my kitchen.
A guy is down on the sidewalk
and the two of them are helping him.
You know, he's drunk.
He split his head open
and they're leaning him against my car.
God forgive me my first thought
Blood all over it.
But he won't go in no ambulance,
he wants his wife or whatever.
I go in the other room.
You know those twigs on that far side?
Where you were working last year?
I just want to take a little rest and then
get out there, tie some twigs into little bundles
for the garbage man—he won't take anything
if I don't tie it up. They take it to that landfill,
remember that time we dumped the sheet rock?
A pit was filled with dogs?
That place.
I don't want to go out of the house,
not while they're there.
So—no one was going anywhere till the ambulance
got there—I thought I'd have a cup of tea.

Anyway, I just sit down
when I look out the window—nobody there.
So I walk to my kitchen door,
next thing I know a taxicab is slowing down.
He must be looking for that guy,
I have to tell him something,
and it was right then.
I thought it was an explosion.
This woman coming up the hill,
she must have been shitface,
comes bouncing off that wall
that big granite, that rock, over there.
Shoots right for the cab.
I think Holy Jesus she's going to kill me.
She hits the cab
          —he lived, he's okay, he had stitches—
and she wedges herself right between
the big pine tree you told me never to cut down
and my front porch. Right between,
didn't touch an inch of my house.
And gets out—you know what she said?
"I'm sorry." "You're sorry?" I said, "Lady!
You're lucky to be alive."
Not a scratch on her, and you know, Michael,
God forgive me but my first thought
when I saw her coming—
and they're only giving me eight hundred,
I should have eighteen for the stress—
but my first thought when I saw that lady coming
—God's punishing me for this—
right for the place where I tie my twigs,
it was "Oh,
a new porch."

Two

The Corn Maiden

In our village when the crop is sweet,
the yellow jubilee strain,
she comes in her flatbed,
and we pull over, late in October
in four wheel drives, on choppers,
in pickups and wagons.
I don't think her traditional worship
became a ploy by the growers ever,
and the farmer didn't hire her
so her tan and the shimmer of gold
over her arms and Nordic shoulders
would stop traffic. But here we are
—mostly husbands, dowdy wives—
picking up corn for the freezer.
We crowd close and almost touch
her thighs dirty from the mound of corn
where in dusty cutoffs she pulls them
ear by ear from between her legs, like birth,
and we go slow, we try to chat,
unpeel each husk till, fire in our palms,
she lifts the coin with broken fingernails,
and smiles—shine of crooked teeth,
dust and sweat coat her bare arm.
But later, much later after moonlight
brushes a ridge of the valley
and younger men lean on their handlebars,
a few sprawled on the tailgate
among the ears and extra bags,
brims of their white Stetsons
filling with moon—only then,
under the ink wash of silver
a smudge of soil on her breast
swaying in the tank top
when we can't pretend to look away,
does her glance fall over us,
the customers, as if we were
Inca priests who wield obsidian knives

to tear out our own hearts
from husks of breath and stone.

Crossing the Sea of Cortes

The Sea of Cortes lifts and rolls.
The body of a whale rides thousands
of swells. Moon touches the horizon,
and we on the M. M. Puerto V.,
we ride these wastes.
Lovers on deck walk like us,
they steal into shadow.
We stand at the rail.

A star is on the Sea of Cortes.

We watch it race, the sudden prey of sharks
upon the waves, until we see it is a hand,
palm up, lying on a swell. It drifts
into the foam, until we see it is a face.

We turn so quickly from the rail
the lovers lift their eyes.

We turn back, and watch it float,
eyes shut, folded in moon.

We make ourselves leave the rail.
The lovers walk before us
to find a place to lie.

Cortes long ago was a god returning,
his hair the prophecy's last detail.

Moctezuma sent a legion of his best.

Hernan Cortes returned each man's right hand.

Now only moon shatters the swells.

The heart of a young man is a thin reed pipe.

In two years he destroyed the Aztecs.

Tonight families lie on blankets
on the floor of the salon.
Why have I come here?

To see a man and a woman
roll and fall into one another,
his hand on her hip?
The morning sun
counts dimes
on their spines.
In waves the light
is a bird, great Condor,
where the lost map floats.

Hibakusha

It is bright midnight. Heat
is against the backs of our necks
as we run. Many are burning
on the road behind us.
A great light from the sky
crushed the house, the city fell down.
We were naked people running,
blackened as barbecue, shreds
whipping behind ourselves.
Our hair burnt, faces swollen,
lips ripped from the teeth.
I could not tell men from women,
the sex organs were burnt off.
My own body was uninjured
and I was in another world.
In the fragmented light
across a footbridge, two horses, dead.
I touched one, it was still warm.
Then I became afraid. I almost stepped
on a woman sitting down, her hands
searching for nipples in her blouse.
I tried to help her, taking her arm,
and all the skin came off.
She had broken legs. I'll carry you,
I said, but a thousand people
were pushing and she was lost.
For months every day I saw them die.
The gums bleed, hair falls out,
then purple spots like snakebites
along the skin. My sister, her mouth
closing around a small cake of coal,
and my husband who had never
been to the dentist. A set of teeth
in perfect condition.
They could have been his.
I buried the teeth in his grave.

The Monolith

I go out there every day where the golden neck
of the browsing workhorse hangs over
rusted barbwire and nudges my fence posts flat.
Out there where a garden used to be,
where March weeds dangle white.
I go out and the neighbor's muddy goat bleating
is tethered to a dry blackberry,
Holsteins stupid as shoes,
graceful as women in leather.
I go there with a sledge
split from head to halfway up the shaft,
so heavy pulling my shoulder down.
A pasture rolls beneath a tangle of stalls,
a tower of truck canopies in clover
and new cut alder, pigpens, a goat hut,
bright pink manufactured home planted
by the creek quiet as hell except
twilight frogs leap in the void.
Out there where I whack a plain steel wall,
and go all day like a tribal drummer,
wake up People!
I could be shooting stray dogs in a pit.
Nobody comes. But in dreams the celebrants
wear black suits and gray vests,
serious hat brims strain their eyes,
the body I've just entered
dressed in my old black suit and tie
printed some industrial design.
I go out there night after night
to slam the wall and hammer my failure.
Not a dent—no rust, not a puff of green
to rot metal where my number burns the dirt.

Aria

The tangled alder bow over the roadside
and the swamp, where they'll fall.
The soprano in the pickup weeps an aria,
wrens outside chorus sunrise in a loop of branches.
Behind a bough of fir, a sudden cry.

The wavy road sprays across a dark wood.

A falling swoop, her tail feather
a flicker in my headlight,
and the eagle glides, her body all wing,
a wiggling rat dangled from a tine of copper talon,
and in three slow strokes, climbs
from the highway to a lighted treetop.

As a witness in the high-pitched
opera of the vaulted grove,
I became a man who kept white feathers
secret all day.

My heart is like that,
laborer with its living captive,
rippling under a cracked ribcage,
singer bursting into morning light.

Kali Bushtit

The ladder bucks and tilts
off squashed blue plums.
The tatter of my hat sheds rain.
Plums the size of eggs
already nestle in the colander.
It's getting harder on my legs
to climb the higher rungs.
I drop one in the crocus
when the crow scouts the ladder,
and face the tent of gypsy moth.
My eyes are off-focus.
I snap the branch, bring it closer
and see—it's a nest,
bobbing in my hand,
mostly moss and lichen thread,
mint patched in askew,
cat hair, feather, wild wool,
wick of candle, string, sad tissue, seed.
Inside, the smell of dirt, a black
garden. I go weak. I am alone.
Shrill cries, scissors on a nail.
On a higher limb, their mother,
an inch of ragged head and tail,
twists on me her one black eye,
bounces on the broken branch.

Dunlins

Their white breasts
turn on wind, mosaics
of fifty, more, fewer
than the year before,
trill on one wing,
zing off a wave,
then light on eelgrass
heaped in thinner cords
than last year's.
They scatter, peck sand fleas,
far fewer now too, three
seconds, five, then
whose idea to swarm
on drafts off waves?
To whiplash till
they wipe each blue
from sky and sleep
—but where?—
to lift off, flash
in dim first light
and vanish.

Happiness

I knew that the swallow
had finished her nest
not when she let go
the fluff of a seagull
and dropped ten feet
to catch it, but when
she did it again.

Swans & the Police

The Trumpeter Swans in a rainy field
by the freeway when the Everett Police car
slips past, all white pieces out of place, stoppers
in the mud holes. A sign warns duck hunters:
"Swans are never in season;
 it is illegal to hunt them,"
and one wonders why it need be told.
Why, for that matter, not told the beauty of ducks
should exempt them, as the camouflaged
greasy beauty of hunters does them,
one lifting a spattered boot
while the other delicately pinches and raises
the barbed wire beside the road
where hundreds of swan lie in the rain,
the Everett Police, one wants to think,
slowing to admire quietly, as Breughel might,
having selected just this moment
for the serf to guffaw at how beauty preens
and flutters in the ravaged corn mud.

Cloud Work

for Robert

Afternoon moons are palest.
This solstice gibbous
led the blue sky
to break open a two week old cloud.
And it's so much work to build them.
I should never complain again.

A loner swan rows across the bottom of the sky,
a broken cornfield, shattered stalks
devastated by December,
and arcs toward the moon ghost
palely loitering in a bough,
face immersed in rain.

But then gives up, veers
back across the mud to the white flock,
trumpeting effortless azure
labors in heaven,
the news of blue.

The Moon & Mount Rainier

1.
Today as the dew
burned off those diamond webs
sagging in spiders' hay,
I saw myself beside a road
that's vanished.
The sun low on the foothills now,
my windshield blind white,
I have few hopes.
Just so the days
pass like geese
startled by cloudburst.
Everything comes back,
trudging over frozen ground
of decades. I could be the girl
thumbing a ride, the boy
behind her in windy light.
Now they're huddled in my back seat.
Christ, they sound so hopeless.
I'm no help. I suggest things
even I would never do.

2.
The moon is a half-opened eye
rolling toward late daylight
up snow slopes.
It is where Mount Rainier belongs,
rising on a clear day
to vanish. We can stop this talk,
my car can drift on its own,
we can watch, and worship.
This is my only home.
Though the decades walk toward zero,
I will bring you to a thing of the road
with feathers the wind has wiped and riffled
where a drop of rain is trembling
the thread a spider built

from weed's tip to feather's
where cars forget us,
where the snow on the moon lives,
and the moon bends
and the crushed face rises
from its smoothed hollows of ice.

Luna

On the porch the big dog thumps
when the moon slides up phantom twin cedars.
A line from my notebook, twenty-five years old,
floats off parched summer trails—
"rises a lady with a candle in her hand."
Memory rushes from the litter
with just one pup bloody and squirming
in her cupped gloved hands.
I saw the birth of fog—out beyond
the argument of garbage and property.
A wave along the tops of poplar,
cottonwood went silver
as the moon breathed the shape of a lake,
tears in its sheer fabric wafting upward
in slightest evening breezes.
Past midnight, the fog draped over a willow,
smeared the bedroom window,
hung from bird pecked barn rafters,
and veiled all but the eyes of the moon.
She shall not be gazed upon by all men.
She is the bride of one master, not one of us.
A voice, keening "oo-la-loo" through the fog.

Whitey & Jessie

Jessie, Jessie angel, like gentle pets
who guard the cradle, the only good dog
the world gave me. Why was Whitey
waiting with his gun in the coop that night?
Or was it poison he put? Not because he was,
as he seemed, a man with a thorn in his soul,
but only that Jessie had come to his rabbits
and somehow caught their feet, while hearts
the size of chestnuts beat like hummingbirds in fur.
Five rabbits, blood coating her jaw,
left mostly puddles in loose straw
under the hutch. The man who begged me
"bring her to town" said she'd never
eat chicken again. When she started in on Whitey's,
then mine, I chained her all day to a banty carcass.
She could get out of any tie-up. She did.
Came always to my hand,
and must have come to Whitey's.
Or did he snap her neck? Whitey with horse-
shoer's hands to keep the gelding still, who could
"Forget about them birds—she's just a bird dog,
can't be helped. And she got yours too? But this
now. This! How can I look at this?"
Whitey's creased and twisted hands,
knuckles gray and flat as nails,
lifted gently the body of rabbit. "No feet."
With such pity he whispered Jessie must not
come near these other, living rabbits, "must not,"
his eyes already on a chestnut mare
to forget this too, brute death, these five.
I saw Jessie go that night and even though
I'd moved across the town, I knew,
but didn't squat down in that rain,
or bring her to my hands
and into wet fur say no, Jessie,
just tonight, lie down, lie down.

Black Dog

The small black dog with the red bandana
waited wave after wave after wave for him,
his board the bone
unburdened by the lean quick sea.
All morning the rollers whose tongues
echo in tide pools among starfish and anemone
translated the master and six others
from families of undercurrents to colleges
of breath to textual misreading of sneaker waves.
The dog couldn't tell who the master was—
something out there in black,
far in the white breakers.
When we spoke to her she ran on
to another empty wave,
silent till the last board came in.
Faith is the language we all understand.
I thought of her just now as we uttered
our first cries in bed in months,
the crest of some dark vision broken,
our mouths spilling over.

Nettle

Stinger. Whip with teeth. Poison tribe
of tiny spine. Guard dog. Foot soldier.
Prong on the iron gate to a mansion of shade.
Spiky key of the vault. Prickles under
the forearm's bright flesh, a trail of sweat,
ice dripping on the rise of breast in wilderness.
Columkille's monk who threw off the cloth
diving past sword fern to scrub his loins.
A four year old's cry in the grove, but
shaggy Yew has shaded down the Dock,
feathery spray with dapple brown
whose juice would sweet the pain.
Stem across the lips of the flamenca.
A wand to brush her hips in private.
Stinging zero's mouth about my nipple.
Needle exploring vines of the heart
withered without the brush of lips.
Long hair when you appear on the trail
to tickle the ankle toward exile.
Tongue-tip lifted to fluff the tent,
to slip into the crease of palm,
bend wrist, touch pulse.

To Curve

for Tim & Mary

Somehow it is the natural way
with women and men
that one is the shadow, one is light.
And a particular light;
let's say the garish bar ambience
that hides in the pouches of the eye,
molds the brow, sculpts a fine cheekbone,
dissolves in the bowl of a throat, later turns
to that predawn formlessness
so unlike sleep I have found myself saying
again—and I'd forgotten—"how
extraordinary, how unreal."

Goodbye and the last juice flower kiss
or handshake, and the stare that almost utters
how I'm trying to fix this face to a memory
so crimsoned with endings, so softened
by last touches and smiles of those
I would have loved
had the turning-into-daylight
not brought the world
to this cleft of a river that goes,
one way to market, one
to the pockets and multitudes
of an estuary.

Only this morning I saw tennis shoes
toeing the plain sand the undertow
might have drained of one
who, perhaps flashing
beside the inconspicuous minnows,
had come here after a life
of simplest deceits
to see this finger of salt
slide to the bottom of a river
to deposit the slightest refugee

to a lit and freshet pool, one
whose own blond fetus
maybe wavers in some mud grass
near the street,
one who couldn't any longer say
"Goodbye, I love..."
whose own mouth takes whatever form
is pressed on it by a strange and salty finger.
And only around the simplest things:
"bone," "toy."
After dinner
we'd been sitting on the clean lawn
with mosquitoes and the moon
in that after hangover serenity
and ordinary vision
of idle people,
when a loud frog grunt
from across the dark of the pond
made us quiet, as had we been overheard, observed,
our pasts and future thrown open,
our two lives seeming to deserve
no further comment.

Three

Driving Home in Fog

Home, the tavern, coast
and these half-spilled bottles
on the truck floor dancing.
Anywhere the home—this fog, this night,
this coast edge run from tavern to tavern.
a gold room, warm, and everybody waving.
Years in the faded look of it. Years.
Never finding the word.
The bottles jiggle by my feet.
This night a home, a fog drunks make lucid,
tired towing the cars of all the nations,
I pass a mare and colt loose in the road.
So right. So assured their place along the shadow.
Stepping light, keeping close.

One Fine Day

Homage to Janos Pilinszky

—it was spring. James Wright's ponies
just across the highway pranced and twisted
and wove the dried grass downhill and uphill.
Shreds of fog in seconds became dawn,
a jet of the blue lake surfacing
behind blurry cottonwood.

From where I watched, they looped round
and around one another, and in silence,
my windshield finally clear, the motor turned off.
How can they live like that, with no rage?

I was listening for the driver I wouldn't see,
but who will be relieved at the last of those five
slow switchbacks where the highway cuts
above their pasture, and who will fire into
the straightaway spill round my blind curve,
and there we'll be—mare and foal dip into dawn
and fog on swift white backs, and me,
window down, pretending to listen to the road,
to think of a reason to go.

The Gatekeeper

It's smoky in the west
where fire fighters work
and pink foothills fall,
one on one to the coast.
Our Amtrak winds by bands
of foxglove, cool fir, smoke
fitted to a cliff-side track.
If I were conductor,
or even gatekeeper at some outpost,
I would love my job.
The heart never rests,
nor the eye, the ear,
and everyone passes, gently
lifting hands as they utter
rich truth in subdued tones.
Through scorched Oregon
cornfields' smoked light,
a canopy-filtered sunset,
we hissed past shadowy
amber hay. Now night commands
these hills to dim, no porch light shines.
The last deep scarlet
on the shoulders of earth
are like my lovely sleeping wife's
red silk shirt. Behind me,
a man and a woman talk
across the aisle about pack-mules
and llamas. Her voice
has barely anything left
of an English accent,
and his is the weary rasp
of a Western American retired
from long-haul trucking.
Soon they'll be asleep,
or else each alone
in the dark seat watching night
fly into hills. They both are careful

not to ask too much.
Even if it weren't so late
in the coast-light smoke,
they would speak as softly,
and even if I didn't know this language,
the way they speak it
would lead me to set everything I own
out in the fire pits and beg
to make sounds as kind as theirs.

Myrtle Lake in the Morning

Water near shore has circled her waist
and her spine rises up,
a leaf shaft in first light.
When she turns it is to beckon me,
her hair and breasts wet.

A friend of many years has died
and I don't share the loss with her
or mark the place that's left.
At a smaller lake than this I wept,
tossing rocks in the water.
Then, suddenly sure,
I threw my watch in their circles.

But nothing has returned, and now
grass green water enfolds her waist,
the sun bends as if to its mirror,
and every bird on earth is ringing.
I hesitate to take a step, but do
and wade toward my lover's hands.

Apology

When the sun wriggled
the thinly leafed maple
a color in mid-dream,
the man I want to be
so you'll forget who I am
stood, and didn't fail
at each turn on a screw,
each glass chip under
your foot, slice
of burnt toast, each dollar
I stop interest growing on,
thinning our account, over-
paying, repaying over
my bad math in the passbook
where the numbers never lie
and we are or aren't talking
about what to let's do
with the money, but I fuck
up again so badly IRS
and old mortgages catch up
(I feel their breath, the guy
downstairs in the Navy's a spy)
and I must make you love me

again, the hero who dreams us
out of this past mistakes hotel.

Dare You

"Let's pretend," she said,
coming down Stampede Pass
"we're a runaway truck,"
dusk on granite and snow.
Why not I said, I'd said
no all day to putting in again
at the Naches rapid
till if I didn't hold her wrist
she'd have gone with only a grin
and no paddle in the smelly raft.
At least we were talking.
So, yes, I kissed brakes
and steering goodbye.
The entire American continent
plunged into the gravel
turnout for runaway semis
up to the axles, headlights,
doors, and when I yanked the hood,
the engine packed with stone
the size of ball-peen hammers
streaked orange as the highway
where passengers in flashing windows
laughed at me. So did she,
hysterical that I went apoplectic
and barefoot in the dying light
from tire to tire
with clam shovels unearthed
from the trunk, two puny spoons
to attack the stones of Mars.

Dust on Stones

I stepped across the street,
afraid I'd miss another sunset
unless I hurried to the leather chair
and the grain of desk, branded in my room
a poppy color light. "Wait for me,"
you called, but I was on our step,
and you were bent to two dark calicos
under heavy locust boughs;
a canopy of white dust spilled
where tree roots split the ground.
I groaned when you rose slowly from the cats,
but a white Porsche shot past, and drove
the feathertail end of evening
up to my face. I worried till your smile
floated past the blur of windshield
and showed you were okay.
You passed me, jiggling keys.
The city seemed to sigh in its dust,
a river stone trapped in sidewalk.
I saw you look back,
and leave the door open.
What if I am dying?
My bones shrinking,
my voice erasing itself.
Across town an engine with a mile of freight
pulled tons of metal south.
The arc of a swallow swept our porch,
a neighbor at a window whistled
the last bars of a country tune,
and you leaned in pale refrigerator light.
I hurried in. I wasn't late.

The Guest

The clicking latch, worn by years of tenants,
woke me. You were asleep, you heard nothing.
But when lights downstairs go on, I'm up from bed,
barefoot on the step. A tall Indian in black
t-shirt, dark river of hair, a wrecked face,
lopes in from the kitchen, eating yogurt.
He holds up his hand, plastic spoon between finger
and thumb. "I'm a friend," he says, "just looking
for a flashlight. Got a flashlight?" I gesture
to the open door; a summer breeze
carries rose and street smells off the porch.
Pitch and smoke and soil rise from him.
I turn off every light from kitchen
to hall, and crouch in the front porch shadow
while he knocks at neighbors' windows,
then by a car's tire shines matches
on gutter bricks, his white yogurt container
in the other hand. I squirm under the rail
and dart past a rose bush to squat half-naked
by the dented door of your Rambler in the drive,
my hand on chrome lit a little by night sky,
bones thin with silvered hair near the knuckles.
He's lighting a new match, his last, I think.
What did he lose? At Neah Bay, friends used to say,
Makah came night and day to borrow
paintbrushes, cigarettes, a match, wine,
cameras if they needed.
I would have been honored to be asked,
would have left the door unlatched.
But I'm not that white boy anymore.
I should be telling you that down his trail
of living rooms and kitchens I followed
and sleep-walked the lit alleys, green dumpsters,
not that I waited till he stopped a block away
for a spoonful more of yogurt
before I stepped out of shadow
and poured my flashlight over the same ground,

not that I knelt to scratch the bricks
and got just the smell of soil,
then locked out the breeze, and fit my shadow
to your body in the wrinkled sheet
and fell almost instantly to sleep.

Metanoia

...the setting up of an immense new inward movement.
Matthew Arnold

When the tide rises
a heron flaps off,
hanging a wing over water,
thin contraption of grace.
I walk out there, into the bay,
the shallows a wild skirt
blowing from my waist,
and lash a twenty-foot fir drift
to my wrist for winter cordwood.
Hawks from the valley
wander over—or I
have walked on to their range.
They're warning me off
in the orange dusk.
Are they frightened
and cry a change of course?
No, I don't know meanings.
I can't even pick up
what my wife drops.
She handles truth
the way longshoremen salvage
dented cans of peach.
I stumble under cargoes
I loaded myself. Or, blind—
as yesterday to the goodbye in the hand
of my friend, thin as mercy
in his final months of AIDS—
my fingers work the rosary
barnacles have strung over the log,
and I believe from the hawk's arc,
when the wing opens,
and the sun shatters,

I am only a thing
in a yellow sweatshirt
tied to a tree.

Yes & No

Nothing matters more than actions.
To Do is a love poem.

Although we do not know each other,
the baby is coming over the hill.
Sunlight ribbons the new knot
of his face, the sea of her eye.

I'm uneasy in the mirrors now.
I can't say Yes Let's Do It
and not think No.
                    All my life
I've wanted not to know the future,
loved surprise, expected guidance
out of accident and agreed to follow.

But now Yes is coming over a hill
to arrange our two lives, a poem
addressed to x or y,
shadows on the chromosome.

It's not easy not to doubt;
this life that is our flesh, inside you,
and laughter and screaming and bone.

Woman with Child

Full as a bell
dug up in the river,
old brass choked with algae,
her feet caked
with the mud of the soft bank,
she walks as if pine needles
cushioned every step,
as if the body were a basket,
borne by a stranger
whose eyes see through
her eyes.

Preparing the Emergency Kit for My Son in Kindergarten

The instructions help me see him with survivors.
When I turn on the news, they pull him
from rubble; each photo is peeled from his skin;
he waves from the stretcher;
a bomb gives up the sleeve of his shirt.
As I roll up the sleep suit, a fireman or nurse
in the dark air pocket or Red Cross bivouac,
reads him our letter. We'll write it tomorrow.
As I choose his toothbrush, the teacher
lines up the boys at white cups
and reminds them that cavities are bad.
When the instructions tell me to zip lock stillness,
I dress him for the wreck, or the flood,
moments before the shooter opens fire.
"Daddy, when there's a earthquake,
are the roads sort of broken all up?"
When I crawl past the freeway ruins,
I find his voice in the panic of phones.
As I fill a jug with clear water, he drinks,
drips down his chin. Drinks. Such thirst.

Playing Catch in Hungary

He wants grounders,
till one takes a wild hop
on ruts in well-trimmed grass,
an opening beneath the oaks.
"They're out of reach," he yells,
and fires above my glove.
I trot to yellow clusters
whose pungency lingers
on my throw, and brings me home
to graves and the rubble of jihad.

"Mit es?"
What's this? "Amerikaiak,"
say the strolling lovers
here in Szeged by the Tisza.
A little boy scurries and dives.
A white flicker in the grass,
a father in the field,
sunset tips the castles orange,
the rebuilt bridge a brassy wave.
Gold mine tailings
Australians paid Romanian
graft to overlook
brought cyanide to Tisza's beaches,
and to their famous bottom fish,
a hundred thousand mouths
of hairy spiky "oh's,"
as Szeged's anglers wept
over their poisoned catch.

He worries he'll be out of shape
next chance up at bat.
They know this, the lovers in the grass.
They see we keep our ways;
if we adopt Hungarian ease,
diamond and pennant will vanish.

They are very young.
It wasn't even their parents
who tried not to know
the millions in Nazi nets.
They're too young for so many zeros.
                                        An older sister,
Stalin's face a paint flake on a web
in her grandmother's story, gives me her hand,
eyes red, lashes glistening.
Vapor trails bloom and perish.
Twelve triggers armored
for an anthill in Jalalabad,
they streak the east and River Tisza.
A bloated sow, belly up,
is drifting down toward Belgrade.

He throws the ball perfectly,
but I'm already tired.
He knows I'll call it quits,
as my father knew,
relaxed in creased khakis
after all those bombing missions,
when boys on bikes rode past
calling me to glass-strewn lots,
my scuffed ball exploding
in the dust beside his mitt.

Rock Pile

This bucket of pebbles
I dumped on the shallow
cat grave. This hard
bent wood I nailed
to hang his bird bell
and fuzzy blue collar.
From his hill
I measured the view.
The tide's broom
on weed-draped stone,
waves little and big
making moan all day.
All for a cat,
or anybody—the knobby ear
inside trees. Compost of pear
was tilth for moths and bees,
who, dead drunk well into fall,
froze in their juices.
I was sitting on those rocks
when the flame from the oil
refinery across the water
came on, with cold stars.

War

Moths patrol the house and prowl
the kitchen window, drawn by untimely dawns
inside fluorescent bulbs. Awakened and alarmed:
the light's off, hazy moon rise mocks the moths;
night immersed in wings traffics in a soft hysteria
which suicides against twin glass doors
so loudly we think to let in the cat,
but a moth undetected slips past
and gallops against the radiant TV,
till the actual cat lunges from the dark,
gasping and snarfling from nasal lymphoma,
and kills it.

Tomorrow they'll maraud again.
So many, so driven they can't be saved
—alike the warlord field mice
clamor and hush in the dog food stash
as half an orange moon ascends Coyote Ridge—
or last week's whale wrong way up Samish River.

One, a casualty stunned by the stealth
of our cancerous cat, detained in the impromptu
barrack of our palms, who dusters and flutters
the smooth bars of fingers, we think to rescue,
and float it deep and free into the cedar ,
into dark, though all it wants is glow,
into safe cool night, though, if it could choose,
it would burn.

Insomnia in Heaven

You get up because the cat is purring in your ear.
You put her out. She doesn't want to go,
but you open the door and she leaps
from your hands, miffed. The big dog too.
Three a.m. Purring so loud in your ear
and then under the chair out of reach
like she was wishing hard hard for that kibble
clicking on the plate.
You could hear her in three different rooms.

Then you lay back down.
You hear this purring sound now
and get up again to put out the other cat.
But there is no other cat.
You put yourself out instead
and try to sleep beside a bowl
half-filled with dog food.

As soon as you dream your lover boy
bounding the fence, ripping fur
from between your shoulder blades,
you hear this purr and wake to put the cat out.
But the house is over there, all lit up,
and the purr comes from branches of alder;
the shed roof purrs, tops of the cars;
fence-posts separate neighbors and purr.
The film of constellations you try to rub
from your eyes returns as the heart and lung
and liver of your own sweet cat
whose purring swells the sky and spins the planet.

Rosehip Plum Cherry

After we fought
I was in a wood,
my hands slashed
from the thorns.
Dry wind lifted
brown broadleaf,
piles of maple.
I was lost,
so I sat on moss
of a nurse log
out of which a fir
had arisen, leaned
to full height
and split, ribboned
for the cut.
The dark was coming.
I began again
through the thorn.
But then I saw
the rosehip
and all the fight
drifted out of me
on a breeze
up the draw
to give you
this red seed,
plump fruit
of the season
I pinched
and carried home.

1.
The plum leaps out of the dirt,
dragging its lace branches.

A large rock, cemented,

plugs the hole where a limb blew away.

Why is a piece of the moon stuck to my window?
Why are dark beads on the glass?
You are only waking up.
Nothing is missing.

Mist still hangs above the barn,
the Great Blue Heron culled from heartbreak.

Clouds take on a lavender shade.
Pumpkins all through one field sprout black hair.

Rewards of the branch,
plums on the snow.

2.
Now the Hungarian Plum,
fruit in the fists of buds,
jangles in cold light
and leads us, its last breath a plum,
back to snow.
Giving itself, defying gravity,
one push and the tree collapses,
craggy in lichen, unthought-of plums
piled in some speculative corner.
Cracked five feet up.

3.
Rain drips down my glasses.
My breath fogs them.
I see this way most mornings.
The world clears before I notice
a break in the cloud, the shutters open,
a woman in nightgown,
breasts spilling,
wipes her eyes.

4.
The snow's crumpling where the irrigation ditch
snakes the mustard field;
a hawk looks up from a few beetles.
Where will he come to in January?
It has already broken out in icy prey.
A single broken stalk trailed a half-moon
before it froze.
Last night the hawk in my headlights rose
out of field grass tall as the hand-lettered sign,
Manufactured Homes. Dwelling on good and evil,
I became this sudden light
thrown where a wing rides on ethics.

5.
I wish I could recreate the moment of surprise
when the white petals swept from the tree
and regret gone with them.
By ones and twos the petals drop.

Caught on a web, one spins and spins.
The whole tree shudders.
I hadn't noticed it bloom and suddenly in a breeze,
one petal, high up, wildly happy.

6.
Long after the man
with the knitted hat
walked his happy dog,
Venus was setting
inside a new moon,
as if an outstretched palm
were about to catch
a silver button
and hide it in a pocket
far below our horizon.

7.
On the window's shade a cherry leaf is silhouetted.
My thumb and finger touch, a petal to look through
at the tavern lit up a block away.
The bartender painted our house.
After his brushes slapped every leaf
and the tree smeared latex on his beard,
he borrowed an ax to hack off all its limbs.

Downstairs now my wife's insomnia
has lit the oven to scrub
and do dishes I would have,
before waking her with morning coffee.
She'll be on the needle now till three a.m. again
setting Noah on a deck with heads of ram,
elk, and snowy eagle
in my father's Christmas quilt.
But for the bobbin all was quiet, the town at peace,
and all night in the kitchen I sat by her side.

Coda
I see your smile—it's light through the window—
open, a witness to last night's poor sleep,
and look at Teddy, head turned and aglow,
blond as the wheat field he's wading in, deep
snores between us, breezes only riffling
the droop of wheat, how waves flutter a sea.
So far from fever he will be waking
soon in language informed by heat, free
to tell his dream: fire engine *and* hot car,
and you see the fever's broken, hold him,
kiss where the virus torched and didn't scar.
All night we sponged and fanned. Was that a dream?
This body of the morning is holy,
torso where we'll burn, and where we marry.

Silhouette

We go out in our skiff on January's moon
in a year already full of sighs and sudden chill,
which means nothing to the eagle
roosting in clutter up a cottonwood,
but the heron squawks and flaps off
from the loony banjo twang in my son's hands,
and in my wife's her grandfather's mandolin.
Pioneers with short paddles,
we skate the hollow shine,
cross the lunar spell with barely a thread,
and that, like breath, slips away.

Michael Daley was born in Boston. He is a graduate of the University of Massachusetts and the University of Washington. After he worked as a laborer, taxi driver, waiter, tree-planter, editor, and Poet-in-the-schools, he became a high school English teacher, and later a Fulbright Exchange teacher in Hungary. Twice the National Endowment of the Humanities has awarded his work, as has the Seattle Arts Commission, Bumbershoot, and the Fessenden Foundation. In 2007 he published *Way Out There: Lyrical Essays* with Pleasure Boat Studio of New York. *To Curve* is his second collection of poetry in 25 years.

Printed in the United States
116694LV00004B/304-345/P